60 KILLER BIGCOMMERCE TIPS & TRICKS

FOR MANAGING YOUR STORE LIKE A PRO

Danielle Mead

Danielle Mead

60 Killer BigCommerce Tips & Tricks for Managing Your Store Like a Pro Copyright © 2017 by Danielle Mead. All Rights Reserved.

Find Danielle Mead online at:
ducksoupecommerce.com
30dayecommerce.com
daniellemead.com

ISBN No. 9781549976216

Printed in the United States of America

CONTENTS

Danielle Mead

INTRODUCTION

Being an entrepreneur can be all-consuming. Friends and family might think owning a business gives you flexibility and the ability to work whenever you want. But in reality, it often means working all the time. It's not a 9-5 job; it's a 24-hour job, where any time not spent working can feel like leaving money on the table.

This book is for BigCommerce store owners who want to manage their stores more effectively. Those who are looking for ways to streamline operations and make the most of the platform so they can get more done in less time. Those seeking a competitive edge to grow their business to the next level.

It's also a great tool for those who set up their store without the help of a BigCommerce partner or expert and therefore never got a full training on all the tools available. Though it's not intended to be a comprehensive manual of the BigCommerce platform, this book is a compilation of tricks I've discovered over the years that many store owners don't know.

You can either read this book straight through from cover to cover or you can use it as a periodic reference, picking it up whenever you're looking for insights on a specific part of the control panel.

Danielle Mead

MASTERING THE CONTROL PANEL

Danielle Mead

#1: USE MULTIPLE TABS OR WINDOWS

Though it's not specific to BigCommerce, using a right-click to open new tabs or windows is probably the most important tip of this book. Even if you don't typically open multiple tabs or windows in your everyday web browsing, you'll want to use this tip when navigating your store's control panel. Why?

There are many situations in managing your store where you'll have sorted content on the page a certain way or filtered the information by certain attributes. Let's say you've searched for products assigned to Brand X because you've received updated pricing from your vendor. If you click on a product, edit the price and click Save, you'll be returned to a list of all products in your store - not just the products assigned to Brand X. Sure, you can redo your search for just Brand X products and repeat the process again and again, but why waste all that time?

Instead, right-click on the first product's name and open it in a new window or tab (I prefer tabs just because they appear at the top of my browser window). Make your product edits and click Save. Now close that tab and voila - you're back to your original search results of Brand X products.

New tabs and windows can also fix a common frustration of the latest BigCommerce control panel main navigation. Rather than utilizing fly-out or pop-down submenus, clicking on a main navigation link like Products will replace the main navigation menu with the Products submenu. This is great until you realize that you need to find an image in the Image Manager. If you click back to the main navigation and click on Storefront (where you'll find the Image Manager), the page will reload and you'll lost the list of products you were working on.

To avoid this issue, right-click on the Dashboard link or the BigCommerce logo atop the left navigation and open a new tab or window. Then you can navigate to the Image Manager without losing your place in your original window or tab.

If you're a Mac user, you may not be familiar with the right-click because many Mac mice have only one button. To mimic a right-click on a Mac, hold down the CTRL button while clicking. You can also adjust your trackpad settings to make a certain corner of the track pad into a right-click.

#2: GET INSTANT HELP

If at any point you have a question or get stuck trying to accomplish a task in the control panel, expert help is just a click away. At the very bottom of the left navigation near your store name, you'll see a little up arrow (^). Click on that and you'll find several helpful options.

First, there's a search box where you can enter keywords and pull up articles from the BigCommerce knowledge base. You'll see instant top results and can click through for more articles if needed.

Next, you'll find a link to the BigCommerce Community, where other store owners and BigCommerce experts (designers, developers) ask and answer each others' questions. If you haven't found an answer in the knowledge base or you need help more specific to your business, the Community is a great place to look for assistance.

Finally, there are two links for contacting BigCommerce technical support - email and live chat. Be aware that tech support reps aren't able to help with design or theme-related issues, but they can answer "how to" questions or resolve technical problems with your store.

#3: CONFIGURE YOUR DASHBOARD

The Dashboard is the first screen you'll see when you login to your store's control panel. By default, it includes four main widgets - Store Performance, Store Statistics, Spotlight and Orders. You can decide which of these widgets you want displayed and in what order by clicking the gear icon located in the upper right corner of the Dashboard.

To hide widgets, simply uncheck the box to the left of any widget name. To re-order widgets, click the icon that looks like a grid of dots to the right of any widget name and drag it up or down in the list. Your changes will automatically be saved for this and all future sessions.

#4: DELAY TIME-OUTS

Tired of the control panel signing you out while you're in the middle of updating a product or processing an order? You can adjust the length of time before your session times out in the store settings.

In the left navigation, click on Store Setup. Then click on Store Settings. Click the Display tab and scroll down to the Control Panel section. Where it says "Timeout Window," use the dropdown to extend the timeout time from 20 minutes to 2 hours (the maximum allowed).

Note: Because BigCommerce is PCI Compliant (complies with laws regulating credit card security), they have to make you re-login every so often to ensure you haven't walked away and left your control panel open for anyone at the library to access (for example). It may be frustrating, but it's worth it to protect your data!

#5: TOGGLE BETWEEN STORES

Do you manage multiple BigCommerce websites? You don't need to manually type in another store's URL to go to its control panel. You can easily switch from one store to another as long as you use the same account to access both stores.

First, make sure you're on the Dashboard or the left navigation is set to the main menu. Scroll down to the bottom of the left navigation and you'll see a link named "Change Store." Click that link and a popup will appear with all other stores you own (or have access to under your current user account). Just click on the store name you want to access to make the switch. There's also a handy search box if your account has access to many stores.

#6: TRACK WORK WITH USER ACCOUNTS

Whether you have a team of people working on your store or you're a solo entrepreneur who occasionally hires contractors to do specific tasks, keeping track of different users' work is essential. If a product is accidentally deleted or an order is updated, you may want to know who was responsible for the change.

I recommend giving every person who works on your store their own user account. This will allow you to track every change they make in the control panel in the case of errors. Tracking work is also important if you're working with an outside designer or developer - you'll want to ensure they are doing the tasks you hired them to complete, while also knowing if they made any changes you didn't request.

To create user accounts, go to Account Settings in the left navigation and then click on Users. When creating user accounts, you can limit the person's access to different areas of the control panel by selecting a pre-made User Role or select Custom to further restrict access.

Once user roles have been created, you can track any user's work in the Store Logs. Go to Server Settings in the left navigation and then click on Store Logs. Click on the Staff Action Log tab at the top of the page to view all work done by all users. To view only changes made by a specific user, click the All Staff dropdown and select the user whose work you want to view. You'll see what actions they took and the associated date on which they made the change.

Note: Store Logs only retain a limited amount of entries. If you and your team are making very frequent changes in your store, your store logs may only show a few days' worth of changes.

#7: INVESTIGATE ERRORS WITH STORE LOGS

At some point, you'll probably get contacted by a customer who is having trouble placing their order. It could be that their credit card isn't accepted or that they're receiving a shipping-related error message.

If this happens, check the Store Logs. Located under the Server Settings menu, the Store Logs are a list of all the events and processes happening behind the scenes of your store. If your store is unable to connect with UPS, for example, that error will appear in the store logs. Or if your payment gateway declined a customer's credit card, you'll see it in the store logs along with a general reason for the declined transaction. Once you have identified the problem, you can follow up with the customer and advise them how to proceed.

You can filter the store logs by type (payment gateways, shipping quotes, marketing channel integrations, etc) and severity using the dropdowns at the top of the log list.

Note: Store Logs only retain a limited amount of entries. If your store processes a lot of transactions, your store logs may only show a few days' worth of events.

#8: MEASURE MARKETING PERFORMANCE

You can't generate sales without traffic, and you can't determine what marketing programs are working without tracking their performance. Whether it's for Google Adwords, an affiliate network, email marketing or another type of marketing, you'll be given "conversion tracking code" during the setup process. This code captures basic information about orders referred by that marketing channel and transmits it back to the channel's internal tracking system.

The directions for most tracking codes will tell you put the code on your store's order confirmation page. But you don't need to actually modify the order confirmation page itself. Go to Advanced Settings in the left navigation and then click on Affiliate Conversion Tracking. Paste the tracking code in the box provided.

If the code has variables that need to be entered, such as the order number or order amount, click the link at the top of the page that says "Learn more about Passing Order Data to Affiliate Programs." This link will open a support article from the BigCommerce knowledge base. Scroll down to the bottom of the article and you'll find a list of the available variables you can insert into your tracking code.

Once you've pasted your tracking code into the control panel and added any necessary variables, click the Save button at the bottom of the screen to complete the process.

#9: CREATE CUSTOM EXPORT TEMPLATES

Need to export orders, products or customer records from your store? You've probably discovered on your own how to export products to make changes in bulk and import them back into the store. But did you know that you aren't limited to the export templates that come with your store?

You can design your own export templates to create custom spreadsheets with your choice of data. Go to Advanced Settings in the left navigation and then click on Export Templates. Click Create an Export Template and then give your template a name. Along the top, you'll find tabs corresponding with the various types of data you can export.

To hide a tab and its contents, uncheck the corresponding box on the main export template screen. Within each tab, check or uncheck the individual fields to include or exclude them from the file.

Back on the main export template screen, scroll down to adjust the settings and format of the data. You can run a test export to see how the information is displayed and then make further adjustments as needed.

Danielle Mead

PRODUCTS & OPTIONS

Danielle Mead

#10: CHANGE PRODUCT LISTING VIEW

As a store owner, you spend a lot of time adding and editing products. Make the main product screen work better for your needs by adjusting the view of the product listings.

On the Products > View screen, look to the left of the page numbers above the product listings. You'll see three little icons - narrow lines, wider lines and a grid. By clicking these icons, you can change how the products are displayed on this important screen.

Beyond the view, you can also change the number of products displayed per page by clicking the default View 20 dropdown to the right of the page numbers. For maximum efficiency, select View 100.

Finally, sort products the way you want by clicking on the headings above each column of information. For example, clicking on Product Sku will sort the products by sku in alphabetical order (A-Z). Click the same Product Sku heading again and your products will sort in reverse alphabetical order (Z-A). The same trick works for the Stock Level, Product Name and Price columns.

#11: SEARCH PRODUCTS MORE EFFECTIVELY

If you've searched for products by name or sku on the Products > View screen, you've likely discovered that the search results can be too broad. Doing a search for "red bag" will return all products with both the word "red" OR the word "bag" in the title. This can make it difficult to zero in on a specific product, especially if you have a lot of products in your store.

Use quotes around words to make your search more specific. By putting quotes around the phrase, you'll pull up only products with those exact words in the product name. You can also enter multiple words in quotes separated by the word AND to pull up products with both words but not necessarily in that order.

Example:
red bag = products with "red" OR "bag"
"red bag" = only products with "red bag" in that order
"red" AND "bag" = products with "red" and "bag" in any order

To search for multiple skus at once, enter two or more skus in the search box separated by commas.

#12: EDIT MULTIPLE PRODUCTS QUICKLY

Sometimes you need to make the same changes to many products, such as when uploading images or enabling Google Shopping. Editing each product and saving it individually can be time-consuming. By using some mouse and keyboard tricks, you can speed up the process and save yourself valuable time.

For this example, let's pretend you've just uploaded a bunch of products using the bulk import tool, but now you need to upload the images for each one. First, go to Products > View and click on the Last Import tab at the top to bring up the products you just imported. Right-click on the first product name and open it in a new tab. Do the same for the next five products. You should now have seven tabs open - your main View Products screen plus six tabs with individual product edit screens.

On the first product's tab, click the Images & Videos tab and upload your image. Don't wait for the image to fully upload to the product. Click on each of the remaining product tabs and do the same thing. By the time you've uploaded the last image, the first product's image will have fully uploaded.

Switch back to the first product tab, click Save at the bottom of the screen and then hold down CTRL+TAB (on a PC) to automatically switch to the next tab. Click Save for that product and then hold down CTRL+TAB to switch to the next tab. Repeat the process until all the products have been saved. Then close all the product tabs.

Back on the main View Products screen, right-click to open the next six products in new tabs and repeat the process. By using this method, you'll fly through your product updates much quicker than editing each product individually.

#13: USE PRICE FIELDS FOR DISCOUNTS

There are four price fields available for each product. Make sure you understand what each field does and how to best use them for displaying product discounts and temporary sales.

The main Price field is your product's default price. If you just have standard products with no discount, this is the only field you need to fill out. But what if your products have a list price and a lower price at which you sell them?

To display products with two prices and have the higher price be crossed out, you'll need to use the Retail Price field. To access this field, click the More Pricing link next to the main Price field. Enter the higher price in the Retail Price field and the price you're selling at in the regular Price field.

If you're running a temporary sale or price reduction and don't need the higher price crossed out, you can use the Sale Price field. The price you enter in the Sale Price field will display as the only price on your website, regardless of what you've entered in the Retail Price and regular Price fields. Using the Sale Price is helpful when you already have a Retail Price and regular Price that you don't want to have to change or re-add once your temporary sale has ended.

#14: MAKE DEPTH THE SMALLEST DIMENSION

If you're using real-time shipping quotes from Fedex, UPS or USPS, you already know that you need to enter weights and dimensions for all your products. But how you enter the dimension information can affect the quotes generated by each carrier.

BigCommerce's shipping calculator (behind the scenes) assumes that all products in an order will be shipping in the same box. It looks at all the products in the order and determines the maximum width (largest Width of a product in the order). Then it determines the maximum height (largest Height of a product in the order). Finally, it adds up all the Depths of the products in the order. Because of this, you'll want to enter the smallest dimension of every product in the Depth field.

For example, let's say a customer orders Product A (dimensions of 10" width x 12" height x 2" depth) and Product B (dimensions of 5" width x 15" height x 3" depth). The shipping calculator will determine that the shipping box needs to be 10" wide (max width of both products), 15" high (max height of both products) and 5" deep (sum of both depths).

If you had entered the dimensions for Product A as 10" width x 2" height by 12" depth, the shipping calculator would determine that the shipping box needs to be 10" wide (max width of both products), 15" high (max height of both products) and 15" deep (sum of both depths). As you can see, the second set of dimensions result in a much larger shipping box, which will result in a higher shipping quote.

Since high shipping costs can be a real turn-off for shoppers, make sure your store is providing the lowest possible rates by always entering the smallest dimension in the Depth field.

#15: USE CUSTOM FIELDS FOR SPECS

Does your store sell products with lots of technical specifications? If so, you'll want to make sure those specs are displayed in an easy-to-read format so that shoppers can quickly digest the information. Listing the specs using a normal paragraph or with bullets can look messy and make the information difficult to scan. Instead, use Custom Fields to create a nicely-formatted table of product specifications.

To add custom fields, edit a product and click on the Custom Fields tab. In the Custom Fields section at the top of the screen, you'll see two boxes - one for the Field #1 Name and one for the Field #1 Value. Enter the spec label (such as Color) in the Name field and enter the value (such as Red) in the Value field. To add more fields, click the blue plus to the right of the value field. You can add as many custom fields as you need.

If you have lots of products with custom fields and find it too time-consuming to add them individually, you can import custom fields in bulk using a spreadsheet. In the export or import spreadsheet, the Custom Fields will be in the last column (furthest to the right of all columns). The format for entering the information will be the label, followed by an equal sign, followed by the value. Multiple fields are separated by a semi-colon.

Examples:
Color=Red
Color=Red;Length=4 feet;Usage=Home or Office

I recommend setting up one product's custom fields through the control panel (as described above) and then exporting that product to see how the information is formatted in the spreadsheet. You can then copy that format and use it to add custom fields to other products in your spreadsheet, ultimately importing it back into your store.

#16: OPTIMIZE RELATED PRODUCTS

You've probably noticed the Related Products section on your product pages. Though the BigCommerce system does a good job of finding products that are related by category or name, you can override the automatic selections and leverage that widget to increase average order size.

To change the related products for any given item, edit that product in the control panel and click on the Other Details tab. Scroll down a little and then uncheck the box that says "Find and display related products automatically". You'll then be able to find products by category and assign them as related products.

Selecting specific related products can be useful for upselling accessories or products that complement the main product instead of those that are similar to it. This type of strategy can help increase average order size by encouraging shoppers to purchase the main product as well as one or two items in the Related Products section.

#17: MAKE THE MOST OF SITE SEARCH

BigCommerce is always adjusting how your store's search box works, and while that may be outside your control, you do have the ability to make your search results more effective.

Every product has a field for Search Keywords which hooks into your website's search box. Many store owners misunderstand this field and think it's related to SEO (search engine optimization) and helping products appear in Google or Bing search results. In reality, this field allows you to control when to include products in your website's search results.

Search keywords have two great uses. The first is for synonyms. For example, if you sell clothing, your products may come in multiple colors. If those colors have specific names like "teal", "aquamarine" or "navy", you can enter the generic color "blue" in the search keywords field to ensure those items come up when a shopper searches for "blue shirts". This is also useful for products that can be referred to by multiple names - you never know which one a shopper is going to use in the search box.

The other cool use for Search Keywords is creating temporary or seasonal collections. Rather than creating a whole category, you can use a unique search term to group products that can be linked to from a banner or social media. For example, you may want to highlight products for summer travel. Add the words "summer travel" in the Search Keywords field for the appropriate products and then do a search on your website for the same phrase, making sure to put it in quotes. Copy the URL of the search results page and you can use it for a carousel banner on the homepage, on Facebook or in an email newsletter. If you don't like the look of the long URL, use Bit.ly to create a short link that masks the full URL.

To add Search Keywords, edit a product and then click on the Other Details tab. You'll find the field in the Other Details section. This field is also available in the product export and import file, so you can easily make bulk updates when you need to add search keywords to many products at once.

#18: USE WARRANTY FIELD FOR CUSTOM TEXT

One limitation of BigCommerce that some store owners find frustrating is the inability to create additional content fields for products. For example, you may want to have a 1-2 sentence overview of the product at the top of the page while keeping the full product description further down. Or you may want to display information like ingredients, a size chart or usage instructions separately from the main description.

There's one field which can be used to display additional product content, and that's the Warranty field. It's unique per product and it accepts HTML code, making it quite flexible in terms of the type of information you can display.

You'll find the Warranty field on the Other Details tab when editing a product. It doesn't have a nice text editor like the product description field, but there's a workaround if you need to add more than straight paragraph text and you're not comfortable with HTML. Simply create your Warranty field text in the product description text editor and then switch to HTML view by clicking the HTML icon located at the far right of the bottom row of text editor icons. Copy the HTML and then paste it into the Warranty field.

Once you've added your content, you'll probably want to hide or change the heading that says Warranty Information on the product page:

For Stencil themes, go to Storefront > Themes, click on Advanced and then select Edit Theme Files. You may need to make a copy of your theme if you haven't already done so. To change the heading from Warranty Information to something else (like Size Charts or Ingredients), click on the lang folder and select en.json. Do a search for "warranty" and replace the text "Warranty Information" with your new text (within the quotes).

For Blueprint themes, go to Storefront and click on Template Files in the left navigation. Scroll down to Panels and click on the plus to expand the list. Scroll down to ProductWarranty.html and replace %%LNG_ProductWarranty%% with your desired heading text.

#19: CUSTOMIZE PRODUCT META TAGS

You've probably heard about SEO (search engine optimization), the process of making your website more friendly for Google and Bing with the goal of having your website's pages appear in their organic (unpaid) search results. While SEO has many components, many store owners overlook an easy way to boost organic traffic.

All products in your store have fields for a meta title and a meta description. The meta title is the main link text that will appear for your product page in search engine listings. By default, this will be your product's name, but you can enter your own text to make the link more enticing to searcher's. The meta description is the text that will appear below the link. If you don't enter a meta description for your products, Google will select text from your product page which may or may not be appropriate or engaging to searchers.

Though customizing your meta title and description won't boost your search engine rankings, it can make people more likely to click on your page, which could lead to more sales. This is because any keywords in your meta title or description which were part of the searchers search term will be bolded.

For example, let's say you have a product with the name "Men's Long-Sleeve Tee - Blue". This shirt may be made of 100% cotton, have a slim-fit and be made by Hanes. If someone searches for "hanes blue cotton t-shirts" and you are using the product name as the meta title, the only bolded word will be "blue". To give yourself a better chance of having bolded (and more visible) words in your meta title, you could enter "Men's Cotton Long-Sleeve Tee | Hanes Slim Flit T-Shirts for Men". This increases your chances of having a relevant page title because it includes a lot more potentially-searched keywords.

The same thing applies to your meta description. You'll want to use that field to include important and enticing information about the product, encouraging people to click. For example:

"Shop our men's Hanes t-shirts for a slim-fit look. This long-sleeve blue tee is made of 100% cotton, pre-shrunk and ready to wear."

You can customize product meta tags by editing a product, clicking on the Other Details tab and then scrolling down to the Search Engine Optimization section. You can also bulk import meta titles and descriptions via the product import spreadsheet. Though adding custom meta title and descriptions can take some time, it's well worth it, especially if you're trying to increase the amount of traffic you get from search engines.

#20: SAVE TIME WITH BULK EDIT TOOL

Need to change a bunch of product prices at once? Or maybe you want to disable a few dozen products. You can export the products, make your changes and then re-import them to your store - or you can just use the Bulk Edit tool.

Bulk editing is available on the Products > View screen and contains slightly different fields depending on if you're using the Channel Manager to sell on Facebook, Ebay or Amazon. But in both cases, bulk editing can be a quick way to make a lot of updates without having to edit each product individually.

When viewing a subset of products, click the checkbox directly under the Add button at the top of the product list. This will select all products on the current page. (If needed, change the number of products per page using the View dropdown above the Action column). Or, check the box next to specific products you want to edit. Then click on the Choose an Action dropdown, select Bulk Edit Selected and click Apply.

The resulting screen will give you editable fields for product name, sku, price, brand, UPC, stock (inventory), categories, visibility and featured status. You can make your changes product by product if each product needs a different value, or you can click the Change All link at the top of some columns to update the value for all products selected. This can be especially useful if you have a group of products that are all the same price but need to be either discounted or have their price increased.

When finished with your edits, click Save & Exit at the bottom of the screen.

#21: APPLY OPTION SETS IN BULK

Did you know you can add or change an option set for multiple products at once? Many store owners aren't aware of this feature, which was added recently without much fanfare from BigCommerce. Still, it's a valuable tool that can save you time, especially when adding new products.

When viewing a list of products, click the checkbox directly under the Add button at the top of the product list. This will select all products on the current page. (If needed, change the number of products per page using the View dropdown above the Action column). Or, check the box next to specific products for which you want to assign or change the option set. Then click on the Choose an Action dropdown, select Apply Option Set and click Apply.

Select the desired option set from the provided list and then click Next. If you have a lot of option sets, you can search for the desired option set by name using the search box provided. Because changing option sets will erase any existing skus and/or rules, you'll need to check two boxes acknowledging you want to make the change. Clicking Next on this screen will apply the option set, so make sure you've selected the correct one!

#22: UTILIZE MASTER OPTIONS

Creating options and option sets are one of the most dreaded tasks most store owners have to undertake. They can seem complicated and are often time-consuming to set up. But by utilizing master options, you can streamline and simplify the process.

Let's say you sell shoes. Some probably come in whole sizes only, while others come in whole and half sizes. You may also sell men's and women's shoes. As you start planning out your options, you start dreading the amount of time it will take to set up so many.

That's where master option sets come in. First, go to Products > Options and click Create an Option. Give it a name like "All Sizes" with "Size" as the Display Name. Next, add your options, starting with the smallest women's size all the way up to the largest men's size, including all half sizes. You don't need to add two versions of sizes like 9 that are available for both men and women.

Next, click on the Option Sets tab. Create a new option set called Women's Shoes Whole Sizes. Add the All Sizes option to your new option set and then click the Edit link next to the option. In the popup, uncheck all the half sizes and the sizes only applicable to men's shoes. Click Save and then Save again to save the option set. Then create an option set for Men's Shoes Whole Sizes, following the same process to uncheck the half sizes and women's-only sizes.

Repeat the process two more times, once for Men's Shoes Whole & Half Sizes and once for Women's Shoes Whole & Half Sizes. Now you've got four option sets but you only had to go through the time-intensive process of adding all the sizes once. Unchecking options is significantly faster than adding individual options, so utilizing master options for different groups of products throughout your store can end up saving you a lot of time in the long run.

#23: USE PLACEHOLDER OPTIONS

Shared options are a great way to save time when creating new products. But they have a downside. If you need to add a choice to just one of the products sharing that option, you'll end up adding the new choice to all products using that option. Sure, you can just create a brand-new option for that product so it no longer uses the original shared option. Or you can use placeholder options.

This trick requires you to think ahead, but it can be worth it for store owners whose products change options seasonally. Some examples would be if you make your own skin care products and like to add seasonal scents or if you make t-shirts and like to introduce new colors for certain products on a regular basis.

Here's how it works. Create your shared option normally, but add a dozen extra "blank" choices at the end of the list. You can give them a display name of "placeholder" or whatever else you'd like. When you create your products and assign the option set, use a rule to hide those placeholder choices. Then in the future, you can easily change one of the placeholder choices to an actual option and disable the rule hiding it from select products.

For example, let's say you sell soap, body wash and candles. All of these products come in three standard scents and share an option with those choices. But you want to be able to have additional seasonal scents only available for the candle. You'd create your option with the three standard scents and then add six placeholder choices. You then hide those placeholders from all the products. When fall comes around and you want to add Pumpkin Spice as a candle scent choice, edit your option and change the first placeholder to Pumpkin Spice. Edit the candle and disable the rule hiding the first placeholder (now Pumpkin Spice). All your other products still have that choice hidden, so you don't have to worry about people ordering Pumpkin Spice soap.

Though this trick require a little more work up front, it gives you a lot of flexibility and can save time down the road, especially if you have a lot of products sharing options.

#24: TWO WAYS TO MAKE OPTIONS OPTIONAL

Sometimes you want to offer upgrades or add-ons to particular products using options. But since these selections are optional, they shouldn't be required for the customer to purchase the product. There are two ways to make an option optional, each with its own pros and cons.

The easiest way to make an option not required for checkout is to add it the option set and then click the Edit link next to it. You can uncheck the box to make the option "not required" for checkout. Most themes show an asterisk or the word "Required" next to required options, so this option wouldn't have either of those indications.

However, sometimes you want the customer to purposefully not select an upgrade or add-on. For example, if you're selling a vanity and the countertop is optional, you may want to force the shopper to turn down the countertop so there's no chance of a return when they receive their counter-less vanity. In this case, it's better to leave the option required but make the first choice "No Thanks" or "No Countertop".

The method you use to display optional options is up to you and should be based on your products and business model.

#25: IGNORE UPCS DURING IMPORTS

Entering product UPCs is required if you plan to sell on Google Shopping or Amazon. But any store owner who has spent a lot of time entering UPCs has likely run into the problem of Excel converting their UPC codes into scientific format. This causes problems when doing product exports and imports.

You can spend time converting your UPC column to text format and then clicking on each UPC to reset it from scientific notation to the correct number. Or you can simply tell the store to ignore the UPC field when you re-import your products to the store.

During the import process, you're shown a screen where each data field from your spreadsheet is matched up with the associated data field in your store. Scroll down to the Product UPC field and change the dropdown from Product UPC to Ignore. When you do your import, the store will ignore that field and your original UPC codes in the store won't be overwritten by the scientific notation versions in your spreadsheet.

#26: SET A DEFAULT PRE-ORDER MESSAGE

Do you offer a lot of pre-order products in your store? You've probably noticed that the default message for pre-order products is "Expected release date is XX," which sounds more appropriate for your favorite band's upcoming album than the summer dress you're selling.

You can change that text each time you set up a pre-order product, or you can just change it sitewide to save time and avoid typos. Go to Store Setup in the left navigation and click on Store Settings. Click on the Display tab at the top and scroll down to the bottom of the screen. You'll see the Default Pre-Order Message field, which you can change to whatever makes most sense for your business.

#27: ADJUST OUT-OF-STOCK DISPLAY SETTINGS

Every store will have out-of-stock products at some point. But did you know you can control how that status is conveyed to your shoppers? You have a variety of choices for marking products and options out-of-stock depending on what you think is best for your business and SEO.

To adjust your out-of-stock display settings, click on Advanced Settings in the left navigation and then select Inventory. In the General Settings area, you'll see options for how to handle out-of-stock products as well as out-of-stock options.

The first setting is for products. By default, your store is set to do nothing when a product's inventory level hits zero. You can choose to hide the product automatically, hide the product from categories and search but leave the product page accessible or redirect the product page to its parent category.

With the first choice, your product will disappear from the front-end of the website and any link to that product page (including bookmarks and links in search engines) will end up on your 404 (not found) page. This can be bad for SEO and frustrating for shoppers. By choosing the second choice, your product page will remain live, but shoppers won't be able to purchase the item because there's no inventory. This is the best choice if the product may be available at a later date. If you know the product is never coming back, your best bet is to choose the third choice, which will redirect the product page to the parent category. Shoppers will then be able to find other items that may fit their needs.

The second setting is for handling product options that are out of stock. By default, the store won't do anything when a particular option's inventory level hits zero. You can either tell the store to hide the unavailable option or leave it visible but mark it out of stock. Neither choice is necessarily better, so it's up to you which one you think is better for your shoppers.

Note that these settings only come into play if you're using BigCommerce to track inventory. If you don't track inventory in your store, you'll need to manually mark products and options as out of stock.

To manually mark a product out of stock, edit it and scroll down to the bottom of the main editing screen. Change the Availability to "This product cannot be purchased in my online store," check the "Show "Call for pricing" message instead of the price" and the type "Out of Stock" in the box provided.

To manually mark an option out of stock, edit the product, click on the Options & Skus tab and then click the Rules tab on the left. Click Create a Rule, select the option and then under Make These Changes, select "Make it unavailable for purchase." You can choose to either hide the option on the product page or show text of your choice.

#28: CONTROL PRODUCT BREADCRUMBS

Breadcrumbs are a set of navigational links that show the path to a page on your website. You've probably seen them on your product pages, displaying something like Home > Category > Product Name. Shopper may use breadcrumbs as navigational links or simply to determine where they are on your website.

However, if you have a small store with a limited number of products or only one category, breadcrumbs may not be very useful. For example, if all your products are in a single "Shop" category, displaying Home > Shop > Product Name doesn't really add anything valuable for the shopper. Plus, breadcrumbs take up space at the top of your product page, pushing more important information further down the screen.

You can disable product breadcrumbs by going to Store Setup in the left navigation and clicking on Store Settings. If you're using a Stencil theme, the options for Product Breadcrumbs will be right at the top. You can choose to show one set of Breadcrumbs or none at all (hide them from the product page).

If you're using an older theme, such as a Blueprint theme (or something even older), you'll find the Product Breadcrumbs setting a little further down on the Display tab. Your theme will give you three choices - to display all breadcrumbs for a product, to display just one breadcrumb or to display none. The first choice means that if a product exists in three separate categories, there will be three breadcrumbs listed at the top of that product page. This can take up a lot of space and also looks messy. I suggest changing that setting to display only one breadcrumb to keep things clean and professional looking.

#29: CHANGE YOUR WEIGHT SETTINGS

Product weights are required if you're using real-time shipping quotes. But if you have lightweight products, you may find yourself spending a lot of time calculating your product weights in pounds, which is the default weight measurement in new BigCommerce stores.

You can change the default weight measurement to ounces by going to Store Setup in the left navigation and clicking on Store Settings. You'll see the Weight Measurement setting in the Physical Dimension Settings section near the top of the screen. Now instead of entering .625 for a 10 ounce product's weight, you can just enter 10.

If your store is located outside the United States, you also have the option of changing your weight measurement to kilograms, grams or tonnes.

#30: FIND ALL ORDERS FOR A PRODUCT

As a store owner, you may want to know how many orders you've received for a particular product over the years. Or you may want to see if there's a geographical trend to where certain products might be purchased.

The ability to view orders for a product is a featured that BigCommerce released some time ago, but didn't widely announce. For that reason, many store owners rely on order exports or Google Analytics to get data on orders related to specific products. But it's much simpler than that!

Go to Products in the left navigation and find the product you want to investigate. From the Action menu (the three dots to the far right of any product), select View Orders. You'll be taken to a screen showing all orders that include that product. You can then open each order to view the customer or geographic details or you can do an export of the orders to do some advanced reporting.

CATEGORIES

Danielle Mead

#31: CHANGE SUBCATEGORY ITEM DISPLAY

If your store has parent and child categories (or subcategories), you can control whether and how products from child categories are displayed when a shopper clicks on the parent category. This setting can be useful in maximizing conversions as well as for creating category landing pages.

To change your parent/child category display settings, go to Store Setup in the left navigation and then click on Store Settings. Click on the Display tab and scroll down to the Category Settings section. You'll see three choices.

Let's assume you have a main category called Women's with three subcategories, Clothing, Accessories and Shoes.

The first option, "Show products from the current category only," means that if a shopper clicks on Women's, they will only see products that have been manually assigned to the category Women's. They won't see any products assigned only to any of the subcategories previously mentioned. This option is really only useful if you want to have a category "landing page" with text, a banner and a few featured products. In this case, I recommend putting some text above the product listing that indicates the displayed products are best-sellers or featured.

The next two options will show products from previously mentioned subcategories if a shopper clicks on Women's, but with slight distinctions. If you select "Show products from child categories if the current category is empty," the Women's category will only show products assigned to the subcategories if you haven't manually assigned any products to the Women's category itself. Be careful with this option if you have multiple people working on your store because someone may assign a product to Women's and then your Women's category will only display that one product (which might lead shoppers to think that one product is all you have).

Selecting "Show products from the current category and its children" is your best bet if you don't intend to have category landing pages. This way, whether you assign products to the main Women's category or any of its subcategories, they'll all appear when a shopper clicks Women's. The shopper can then narrow their results by clicking on a subcategory.

#32: CONTROL CATEGORY PRODUCT SORT

Have you ever wished you could change the default order in which products were sorted on your category pages? You can! This feature was released some time ago, but many store owners don't know it's available.

First you'll want to change your storewide default sort. This is the sort order which all categories will display products unless specified otherwise. Click on Store Setup in the left navigation and then click on Store Settings. Click on the Display tab and scroll down to Category Settings. You'll see a setting for Default Product Sort. By default, it's set to Featured Products, but you can change it Newest Items, Bestsellers or something else.

Next, you may want to override that sitewide setting by changing the sort for select categories. For example, maybe you have a New Products category - you may want that to display the newest items first. Or maybe you have a Sale category - you may want that to display the lowest price items first.

To change a specific category's sort, go to Products in the left navigation and then click on Categories. Edit a category and scroll down to the Default Product Sort option. Here you can change the sort order for just this category.

Note: If you plan to use the Sort Order field for products to manually determine their position on the category page (see tip #33), you'll need to leave the default sort at Featured Products. Any sort order values entered for products will be ignored if you set the category sort order to anything other than Featured Products.

#33: CHANGE INDIVIDUAL PRODUCT ORDER

Beyond changing the overall sort method of your categories, you can manually control the placement of individual products if so desired. Unless manually changed, all products have the same sort order, meaning they have no particular sort order and will display in the order determined by your category sort settings.

But you may want more precise control of where your products appear on category pages. Though it can be time-consuming to manage, some store owners like to implement advanced merchandising strategies by utilizing the product sort order.

Here's how it works. Each product has a number assigned to it in the Sort Order field. By default, that number is 0 for all products. If you change that number, the products will display in any category from the lowest sort order number to the highest. The Sort Order field also accepts negative numbers, so a quick way to move a product to the top of a category is to give it a Sort Order of -1, which is lower than the 0 assigned to all other products.

Some store owners want to group similar products together within a category. To achieve this, give each product type the same number. For example, within your t-shirt category, you could give all red shirts a 2, all blue shirts a 3, all green shirts a 4 and so on. One store owner sold tickets to events and wanted the soonest events to appear at the top of the page, regardless of when she set up the product. She could give each product a sort order of the event date. So an event on January 15, 2017 would have a sort order of 011517 and an event on June 28 would have a sort order of 062817. Make those numbers negative and the products will be listed from the latest date to the soonest.

To change the sort order for a product, edit it and then go to the Other Details tab. You'll find the Sort Order towards the bottom of the Other Details section.

#34: FIND PRODUCTS IN A CATEGORY

This is such a simple trick, but I've found that many store owners don't know it! If you want to find products within a certain category, go to Products in the left navigation and then click on Categories. Locate the category you want (you may need to expand parent categories if you want to find products within a subcategory) and the look over to the right for the Action menu (represented by three dots). Click on the Action menu and select Products. This will take you directly to a list of just products within that category.

#35: TURN BRANDS INTO CATEGORIES

BigCommerce comes with a built-in Brands feature, which allows you to assign brands to products and then display those brands on the product page and in menus around the website.

However, brands have limited functionality compared to categories. For example, you can't add a description to a brand like you can with a category, and brands can't be nested like categories to create sub-collections. Plus, some discount rules and coupons only work with categories.

To get around these limitations, make categories for all your brands. Then, create 301 redirects from each brand page to your new brand category. This will allow you to continue using the built-in Shop by Brand menus and ensure that shoppers land on your new brand category if they click the brand name on a product page.

To create 301 redirects, go to Server Settings in the left navigation and click on 301 Redirects. Click Add Redirect and put the original brand page URL in the Old URL field. Select Dynamic Link for the Redirect Type and then click the provided link to find and insert the new brand category you set up.

#36: CATEGORIES AS ORGANIZATIONAL TOOLS

We think of categories as being navigational elements for shoppers to find products. But there's no rule that says you as a store owner can't use categories to organize products in the control panel for other purposes. Because categories can be hidden from the front-end, you can utilize them for a variety of purposes unrelated to navigation.

For example, you might be importing a new batch of products that you know will need additional fine-tuning from within the control panel before going live. Create a new category called "Working" and make it hidden so it doesn't appear on your storefront. Then add the Working category to the category field in your import spreadsheet along with the other categories in which the products will ultimately be found. (To add a product to multiple categories, separate the categories with a semi-color in the Category column of your import file). After import, you can easily get back to your "working" products by using trick #34. Then as you finalize each product and make it live, simply remove it from the Working category on the edit screen. When your Working category has zero items in it, you know you've finished editing and activating all your new products.

Another way to use categories is for targeting coupons and discounts. You may want to offer 10% off with a coupon, but some of your vendors won't allow discounting. You can't restrict coupon usage by brand, but you can exclude certain categories from a coupon. Simply create a hidden category for that vendor's products and exclude that category when setting up your coupon. Or use a hidden category with select products to apply one of the advanced category-based cart-level discounts.

#37: SECRET PROMOTIONAL CATEGORIES

Many store owners, especially those with fashion-focused stores, need temporary categories based on seasonal or holiday-specific products. For example, you might want to create a Valentine's Day category or an Autumn Getaway category in your women's clothing store.

These categories may not fit nicely into an existing category. Valentine's Day products may include dresses, tops, shoes and handbags, so you can't make it a subcategory. You'd have to make it a stand-alone category that will appear in your main menu, but what if you don't have room in your main menu? You can't hide it, because that will make it inaccessible on your storefront even if you're linking directly to it from an email or a homepage banner.

The workaround? Make it a subcategory of a hidden category. First, create a category called Features and make it hidden. Then create your Valentine's Day category and make it a subcategory of Features. Since your Valentine's Day category is not itself hidden, it will still be accessible for linking from emails, banners or social media. But it won't appear in the main menu because its parent category is hidden.

You can add as many seasonal subcategories to your hidden Features category as needed, even re-using them over the years.

CUSTOMERS

Danielle Mead

#38: EDIT CUSTOMER ACCOUNT FIELDS

Whether your customers will be creating an account on the Create an Account page or during checkout, you may want to collect more information than what's available by default in your store.

The standard account form includes just email address, password and shipping address. But what if you're a wholesale company that sells to retailers? You probably need to collect the customer's sales tax ID or business license number to ensure they can legitimately order from you. Or maybe you want to learn how your customers heard about your company.

You can add fields to the new account form to collect whatever additional information you'd like. Go to Advanced Settings in the left navigation and then click on Account Signup Form. Make sure you are on the Account Signup Fields tab. Click on Create a New Field and select the type of field appropriate for your questions (dropdown, text box, etc). Fill out the display name, select whether the field is required and then click Save.

From this screen, you can also edit the display names of existing for fields. For example, if you'd prefer the signup form say "Email" instead of "Email Address," you can edit the Email Address field and change the display name. Advanced users can also assign CSS classes to individual fields so that they can be controlled separately from with your template's CSS file.

#39: GET CREATIVE WITH CUSTOMER GROUPS

If your store is on the Plus Plan or above, you'll have access to a feature called Customer Groups. Customer Groups allow you to segment customers so that you can treat them differently. The most common use for customer groups is separating wholesale from retail customers so that you can give wholesale customers access to case-pack products or allow them to purchase at wholesale prices.

But you can use customer groups for a variety of creative purposes. Here are some ideas to get you going:

Give your best customers exclusive discounts.

Create a VIP group with a discount on all or select products in your store. You could market VIP status as something shoppers can earn after placing a certain number of orders, or simply reward customers who have purchased frequently by reaching out directly and letting them know they've earned VIP status.

Offer a Free Shipping subscription similar to Amazon Prime.

Create a product called "Free Shipping for a Year" and sell it for whatever price you'd like. Create a Free Shipping customer group and then set up a cart-level discount that gives free shipping to only people in that group. When someone purchases the "Free Shipping for a Year" product, add them to that group.

Give certain customers a "first look" at new products.

Create a category named "Preview" or "First Look" and then create a customer group with a similar name that has access to that category. Make sure to uncheck that category from your default customer group so that regular shoppers can't access it. Then use whatever promotional method you want to reward shoppers with "First Look" access. It could be ordering a certain amount, placing a minimum number of orders, taking a survey, sharing content on social media, etc.

Customer groups can be a powerful promotional tool if you think outside the box!

#40: LOGIN TO A CUSTOMER'S ACCOUNT

Have you ever been on the phone with a customer who is having difficulty navigating their account? Maybe they're trying to update their password or find the tracking number for a recent order.

To make things easier for you, go to Customers in the left navigation and search for the customer's name or email address. When you've located the customer's record, click on the Action menu (looks like three little dots) and select Login. This will open the customer's account on the storefront in a new window. You'll be able to see their orders, account information and everything else they can see - as if you were them. By looking at the same screens as your customer, you'll be better able to give them instructions for whatever they're trying to do.

#41: QUICKLY EMAIL A CUSTOMER

Need to contact a customer by email? You don't need to manually copy and paste their email address from the control panel into an email in Outlook or Gmail. Simply click on the customer's email address and a new email to them will automatically open in your default email program.

You can use this trick when viewing customer records in Customers > View and when viewing individual orders under Orders > View.

#42: GET NOTIFIED OF ORDER MESSAGES

The BigCommerce order messaging system is a cool feature that not many other e-commerce platforms include. It allows customers to send messages about their order when logged in to their account. But it has a downside. There is no ability to turn the feature off, and for many years, there was no notification to the store owner if a customer sent an order message. So if store owners didn't check their control panel regularly, they would have no way of knowing that a customer had sent an order message.

Though there's still no way to disable order messaging (without changing your template files), BigCommerce did recently roll out a way to be notified of new order messages. They didn't announce this widely and the control panel doesn't make any mention of it directly. However, if you go to Advanced Settings in the left navigation and click on Order Notifications, you'll see the option to enable email or SMS notifications. In the past, these notifications have only gone out when a new order was placed. But now, they will also be sent if a customer sends an order message.

As of this writing, BigCommerce hasn't updated that control panel page to let store owners know about the order message notifications, but hopefully they will soon.

ORDERS

Danielle Mead

#43: GET COPIED ON ORDER CONFIRMATIONS

When you first launch your BigCommerce store, it's exciting to login to your control panel each day and see if you've gotten any orders. But as time goes on and your business grows, it's easy to forget about signing in to the control panel if you don't have other work to do online.

You can get notified not only when a new order is placed, but also of the order details, by adding a notification in the store settings. Go to Store Setup in the left navigation and click on Store Settings. Then click on the Miscellaneous tab. At the top under Email Settings, check the box that says "Yes, forward order invoice emails to" and then enter your email address. By enabling this feature, you'll receive a copy of every order confirmation email your store sends to a customer. You can include multiple email addresses separated by commas. However, please note that distribution list email addresses (those that forward to a list of other emails) won't work here.

#44: CUSTOMIZE YOUR ORDER STATUSES

When a new order is placed, its default status is "Awaiting Fulfillment." Over the years, many store owners have found this order status to be confusing to customers. But until recently, there was no way to change it.

Thanks to a new feature BigCommerce rolled out, you can now customize all the order statuses in your store. For example, if you sell custom embroidered pillows, you may want the default order status to be "Preparing for Embroidery". Then instead of "Awaiting Shipment", you might want to have an order status of "Embroidery Underway".

To change your order statuses, go to Orders in the left navigation and click on Order Statuses. You'll see a list of all possible order statuses along with their definitions and when their associated emails are sent out. Click the Edit button at the top of the page to change any or all of the order statues to better match your business.

If you want to disable emails for specific order statuses, go to Advanced Settings in the left navigation and click on Checkout. Scroll down to the bottom of the screen and uncheck the box next to any status email you don't want to be sent out to customers.

#45: PERFORM ORDER UPDATES IN BULK

Once your store starts getting a lot of orders, you may find the process of updating them to be quite time-consuming. But you can handle many typical order updates in bulk by using the Action menu on the Orders > View screen.

When viewing the list of orders, select specific orders by checking the boxes to the left of them or click the box under the Add button to select all orders on the page. Then click on the Choose an Action dropdown above the order list and select an action to apply to all the selected orders. You can print invoices or packing slips, capture funds (if you're not capturing them automatically at checkout), export orders to Excel or change their status. Once you've made your choice, click Confirm to apply the action to the selected orders.

#46: FULFILL FASTER WITH A CUSTOM VIEW

If business is booming, you've probably got a lot of orders appearing in your control panel. It's easy to miss orders that need to be processed or shipped because the order date is just one field on the orders screen.

To make life easier, you can create a custom view that just displays the previous day's orders. This will allow you to quickly see what orders need to be processed and shipped out the door.

While on the Orders > View screen, look among the tabs across the top and find Custom Views. Click on that tab and then click the link to Create a New View. You'll be taken to a screen that looks like the order search screen, but at the top, there's a field for the custom view name. You can name this view something like "To Ship" or "Yesterday's Orders" - whatever makes sense to you. From the Order Status dropdown, select Awaiting Fulfillment. (If you've customized your order statuses, select whatever order status corresponds with newly placed orders.) Then scroll down to the Search by Date section and select Yesterday from the Date Range dropdown. Click Save at the bottom of the screen.

Moving forward, you can now click on Custom Views from the orders screen and then select your custom view for yesterday's orders.

Take advantage of custom views to make your order processing more effective. For example, you can also use custom views to create filters for orders with expedited shipping that need to be processed first each day.

#47: RE-SEND ORDER CONFIRMATION EMAILS

Every time a new order is placed, your store sends out an order confirmation email to the customer with their order details. Did you know that you can re-send this email from the Orders screen?

There are two main reasons to re-send order confirmation emails. The first would be if the customer didn't receive it and contacts you wondering if their order was indeed received. The second would be if you need to change an order, either because an item is out of stock or if the customer requests a change (maybe they ordered a size medium when they really need a size small). If an order has been changed, it's a good idea to re-send the order confirmation email so the customer can see the changes that were made.

To re-send an order confirmation email, go to Orders in the left navigation and then find the order in question. Click on the Action menu to the right of the order (looks like three little dots) and select "Resend Invoice."

#48: CREATE AND SAVE DRAFT ORDERS

If you take orders over the phone or sell wholesale, you've probably encountered a situation where being able to create and save a draft order would be helpful. Maybe the customer needs to get the company credit card or maybe they need to get authorization before placing the order. Maybe the customer just got interrupted during their phone order and needs to call you back.

Draft orders are a new feature BigCommerce released in 2017 based on store owner demand. If it applies to your business, it's a feature that will save you lots of time and allow you to provide better customer service.

To create a draft order, go to Orders in the left navigation and then click on Add. Enter the customer information and add products the same way you'd normally create a manual order in the control panel. But when you get to the final screen, select Create Draft Order in the Finalize section instead of selecting a payment method. Then click Save & Create Draft Order at the bottom of the screen.

Once a draft order has been created, you can access it by going to Orders in the left navigation and then clicking on Draft Orders. You'll see a Draft Order URL which you can copy and paste in an email to the customer. By clicking on the link, the customer will be taken to a saved cart with their draft order so they can complete the purchase themselves. Or you can click the Action menu (looks like three little dots) and edit the order to complete the order process once the customer is ready.

If a customer no longer wants to complete a draft order, you can delete it under the Action menu.

#49: ARCHIVE ORDERS TO ELIMINATE CLUTTER

Over time, your orders screen is going to fill up, resulting in pages and pages of orders. To keep your order screen uncluttered and allow you to better focus on your daily order tasks, you can periodically archive cancelled, declined and test orders.

Archiving an order simply removes it from the main orders screen. You can't delete orders from your BigCommerce store, so this is the best way to remove orders from the standard view.

To archive an order, go to Orders in the left navigation. Find the order(s) you want to archive and check the box to the left. From the Choose an Action dropdown at the top of the order list, select Archive Selected and click the Confirm button. Your newly archived orders will disappear from view.

To find previously archived orders, look for the More tab along the top of the screen and click on it to find and select Archived. You can also search for archived orders by clicking on Search in the left navigation when viewing the orders screen. On the search page, archived orders are referred to as "Deleted Orders" since BigCommerce didn't update the language after it changed the name from "Deleted" to "Archived". In the past, you could "delete" orders, but they still remained in the system, which is why they changed the name.

#50: USE NOTES FOR CUSTOMER SERVICE

You probably know that customers can enter comments when placing an order, but did you know that you can also put comments in that field? Beyond that, BigCommerce gives you a separate Staff Notes field for entering comments that can't be seen by the customer.

To view or add order comments, go to Orders in the left navigation, locate an order and then click on the Action menu for that order (looks like three little dots). Select View Notes and you'll see the Comments field in the subsequent popup. This field is great for recording customer-requested changes because the customer will be able to see any notes entered here when viewing the order in their online store account.

If you want to leave notes that aren't visible to the customer, use Staff Notes, which can be found in the same View Notes popup. The Staff Notes field is perfect for leaving yourself notes about changes you made to an order or leaving instructions for another team member who might be working with the order later.

#51: QUICKLY LOCATE TRACKING NUMBERS

Providing top-notch customer service is essential to sustaining and growing your business. If customers call or email asking about the status of their order, you'll want to find any associated tracking numbers quickly so you can give them an update in a timely manner.

The fastest way to locate shipment tracking numbers is by going to Orders in the left navigation and clicking on Shipments. Search for the customer's name and you'll see the tracking numbers for all their shipments. By clicking the plus to the left of the shipment number, you can see what specific item or items were in that particular shipment. This is especially helpful if you often do partial order shipments.

Though you can also find tracking numbers within the normal Orders > View area, they don't clearly show which items were in each shipment. You'll need to click on a shipment link within the order - that will take you to the Shipments page mentioned above where you can see the full shipment details.

#52: SET YOUR PAYPAL RETURN URL

Paypal Express Checkout is one of the most popular secondary payment gateways with BigCommerce store owners. It allows any shopper with a Paypal account to bypass the standard store checkout process and instead use the address and payment information in their Paypal account to complete their order.

However, once a shopper finishes paying on the Paypal website, they are not automatically returned to your website. Though there is a link on Paypal that will take customers back to the store, it can be easy to miss. The problem with this is any order that doesn't end on your BigCommerce store's order confirmation page will be considered "incomplete" and will not appear as an order that needs to be shipped. Because of this, shoppers who have submitted payment on Paypal may receive your store's abandoned cart emails, leading them to believe they need to place the order again. Paypal orders that don't finish on the order confirmation page also won't trigger any conversion tracking you might have set up for marketing programs.

You can avoid these problems by setting the "return URL" in your Paypal account. Login to your Paypal account and click on your profile icon in the upper right corner of the screen. Select Profile and Settings, then click My Selling Tools. Next to Website Preferences, click Update and then enable Auto-Return. In the box provided, enter the URL of your store's order confirmation page.

If you have your own SSL certificate installed, the URL will be "http://yourdomain.com/finishorder.php". Make sure to replace "yourdomain.com" with your actual domain in the URL.

If you don't have your own SSL certificate installed, the URL will have the same first part as your control panel's URL along with the finishorder.php at the end, something like "https://mystore.mybigcommerce.com/finishorder.php".

Make sure to save your changes in Paypal when finished.

#53: AVOID GIFT CERTIFICATE FRAUD

Gift certificates are a great feature, especially for stores selling often-gifted products. However, online gift certificates can be a magnet for fraud. By changing the default gift certificate settings in your store, you can minimize the chances of getting hit with unwanted chargebacks.

Because gift certificates are sent immediately to the recipient upon purchase, scammers are known to buy gift certificates with stolen credit cards and then quickly turn around and use the gift certificate to purchase products from your store. Store owners, not realizing what has occurred, ship the orders out normally.

Then, a few weeks or months later, they receive a message from their payment processor that the original payment for the gift certificate itself has been reversed. This leaves the store owner without the products they shipped (when the gift certificate was redeemed), and without the money paid for the gift certificate itself. Meanwhile, the scammer has the products and can sell them online for 100% profit.

To minimize this type of fraud, you have two options. You can disable gift certificates entirely by going to Marketing in the left navigation and then clicking on Gift Certificates. Or you can make your gift certificates less appealing to scammers by changing the available gift certificate amounts.

By default, your store is set to accept gift certificate values of $1 to $1000 - the purchaser can enter any amount between those two amounts. However, you can change the setting to "Specify a list of allowed gift certificate amounts" and then type in a few set values like $25, $50, $75 and $100. Since fraudsters are looking to get the largest possible return for their efforts, they are less likely to pull this scam for only $100 in free merchandise. Additionally, you'll have a much smaller loss should scammers target your store.

#54: OPTIMIZE YOUR ABANDONED CART EMAILS

Even if your store has a high conversion rate, you're still losing a lot of potential sales during the checkout process. Shoppers may not be 100% convinced they should buy or they may simply get distracted while in the process of ordering and forget to come back.

Abandoned cart emails are a great way to remind shoppers they didn't complete their purchase and encourage them to come back and finish their order. If you're on the Plus Plan or higher, your store includes the abandoned cart email feature and they are enabled by default. Most store owners don't realize they can customize these emails to make them more effective.

To edit your abandoned cart emails, go to Marketing in the left navigation and then click on Abandoned Cart Notifications. You'll see three emails, each set to be sent after a certain amount of time has passed since the shopper abandoned their order. Click on the Action menu (looks like three little dots) for each email to change it. On this screen, you can update the subject line of the email or the email text itself to better match your store's personality, add a coupon code to further entice the shopper and change the delay time for the email. Don't forget to save your changes when done.

From the main abandoned cart notifications screen, you can disable messages if you want to send fewer follow-up emails, or you can add new messages if you want to send additional emails.

To check the effectiveness of your abandoned cart notifications, go to Analytics in the left navigation and click on Abandoned Cart Recovery. By testing the number, frequency and content of your abandoned cart emails, you can optimize them to produce the best results.

SHIPPING & CHECKOUT

#55: CUSTOMIZE ADDRESS FIELDS

When shoppers create an account in your store, they'll need to provide an address. If you're using the standard one-page checkout in your store, these same address fields will appear during checkout. You can customize these address field names and even add your own fields to better match your store and business needs.

For example, you may want to change the "Suburb/City" field to simply say "City". Or if you're selling outside the United States, you may want the "State/Province" field to just say "Province".

To edit the field names, go to Advanced Settings in the left navigation and click on Account Signup Form. Click on the Address Fields tab at the top of the screen and you'll see a list of all the standard address fields. To edit an existing field, click the Action menu (looks like three little dots) to the right of any field and then select Edit. Change the field name value to your preferred text and click save. Please note that required fields cannot be made optional.

You can also add your own fields to the address form. For example, maybe you want to add a field for Delivery Instructions so that customers can indicate if there's a front-door code or specific location where packages should be left. Click on Create a New Field and select the appropriate field type (dropdown, text box, etc). Fill out the display name, select whether the field is required and then click Save.

Note: Any fields you add to the address form will appear in both the shipping address and billing address sections during checkout. Editing address fields is not currently possible for BigCommerce's new optimized checkout.

#56: CHANGE CHECKOUT SETTINGS

The checkout process is the most important part of your website. Some store owners don't realize that they can change a variety of checkout settings to fit their business model.

Go to Advanced Settings in the left navigation and then click on Checkout. First, you can choose the style of checkout enabled for your shoppers. Next, you can determine whether or not to allow guest orders, if customers should be able to add comments to their orders, whether customers must accept terms and conditions to checkout and if orders can be split among multiple shipping addresses.

If you're using the new optimized checkout on a Stencil theme, you can make changes to your checkout's appearance, including the logo and colors, in the Checkout Styling section.

Finally, you can select which order status emails you want enabled. Learn more about order status emails in Tip #44.

#57: SET YOUR DEFAULT "SHIP BY" SHIPPING RATE

If you charge shipping based on the order amount or total order weight, you're likely using the "Ship By" shipping rules in your store. Many store owners correctly set up their weight or order amount tiers with the associated shipping cost, but forget to set the Default Shipping Cost.

Let's say you charge shipping based on the order total like this:

Orders $0-$25 = $5 shipping
Orders $26-$50 = $10 shipping
Orders $51-$100 = $15 shipping
Orders $101-$300 = $30 shipping

Then let's say a shopper places an order for $500. What do they get charged for shipping? That's where the Default Shipping Cost comes in - it's the amount your store charges for any orders above the last tier you've entered.

Unless your store is configured to offer free shipping for orders above your highest specified shipping tier, make sure you've entered a default shipping cost to "catch" those orders and apply the shipping charge of your choice.

#58: SET BACKUP RATES FOR REAL-TIME QUOTES

Real-time shipping quotes are popular with store owners because they ensure that the cost of shipping an order is covered by what the customer pays for shipping. You might be using USPS, UPS or Fedex real-time shipping quotes in your store, but you may not realize that all three carriers have a maximum package size for generating online shipping rates.

Typically, store owners only notice this issue when a customer contacts them saying that they can't check out. They have received an error message stating the order can't be shipped to their location. But the error message is deceiving because it's a generic error that appears any time there is a problem accessing shipping quotes for an order.

Since your BigCommerce store assumes that all items in an order are shipping in the same box, it's not uncommon for large orders to exceed a carrier's maximum allowable size. To ensure large orders don't result in errors, you should set up flat-rate or ship by weight tiered shipping rates that kick in when the real-time quotes are no longer an option due to the order's size.

To determine how to best set up and charge for shipping on larger orders, check your carrier's website for their maximum single shipment limits.

#59: CREATIVE USES FOR HANDLING FEES

Handing fees are somewhat of a dirty word when it comes to e-commerce. But in BigCommerce, handling fees can be combined into the same checkout line item as the shipping charge, making them invisible to the shopper. Therefore, you may want to incorporate handling fees if it makes sense for your business.

One common use for handling fees is to cover the cost of the shipping box and packaging materials. Even if you use real-time shipping quotes, that only pays for the actual cost of shipping. By adding a handling fee of $2 to each order, you can recoup some or all of the packaging costs you'll incur when shipping out an order.

Some store owners want to charge more for the first item in an order than for subsequent items, because it can incentivize shoppers to purchase more products. For example, you may want to charge $4 for the first item and only $2 for each additional item in an order. BigCommerce doesn't have built-in shipping rules to set up these types of charges. However, you can set up a flat rate shipping rule of $2 per item and then have a handling fee of $2. Since the handling fee is only charged once per order, you're effectively charging $4 for the first item and only $2 for each extra item.

Handling fees can also be charged on digital (non-shipped) products. This may be appropriate if you're selling personalized downloadable products or services that you've set up in your store as digital products (because they don't require shipping).

To set up handling fees for shipped orders, go to Store Setup in the left navigation and click on Shipping. Edit a shipping zone and then click the Edit button in the upper right corner of the screen. In the popup, click on the Handling Fee tab and choose whether to charge the same handling fee for all shipping methods or to charge different handling fees per method. Unless you want the handling fee to appear as a separate line item during checkout, uncheck the box that says "Show handling fee separately in checkout."

Handling fees for digital products can be set by going to Advanced Settings in the left navigation and clicking on Checkout. Scroll down to the very bottom of the screen and check the box that says "Yes, apply a handling fee to orders containing digital products."

#60: SET UP WHOLESALE PAYMENT TERMS

If you sell to wholesale customers, you may already have existing payment terms that you want to incorporate into your store. For example, your customer may have Net 30 payment terms which allow them to pay by check up to 30 days from the purchase date.

To create custom payment terms, go to Store Setup in the left navigation and then click on Payments. Scroll down to Offline Payment Methods and click on it to expand the list of options. Click the Set Up button for either Check or Money Order - they will both work for this situation.

On the next screen, change the display name of Check or Money Order to your custom text, such as Net 30 Terms. If you want to limit this payment option to customers in specific countries, you can choose them from the list by holding the CTRL key down while clicking on individual country names. Or you can leave it at All Countries. In the Payment Information box, type any necessary instructions or additional notes that you want customers to see on the order confirmation page and in their order confirmation email. Click Save at the bottom when finished.

FROM THE AUTHOR

Thank you so much for reading this book. If you found it to be a valuable resource, please help me spread the word by sharing it with friends or colleagues who might find it useful.

If you have a moment, I'd also really appreciate your writing a short review of the book on Amazon to share your thoughts with other potential readers. Reviews are the lifeblood of independent authors and give us the feedback and inspiration we need to keep writing.

Feel free to reach out to me anytime at danielle@ducksoupecommerce.com or through my website at http://ducksoupecommerce.com. As an active member of the BigCommerce community and general e-commerce enthusiast, I love connecting with store owners and entrepreneurs.

ABOUT THE AUTHOR

Danielle Mead is a BigCommerce certified partner, e-commerce expert and startup veteran. She is the owner of Duck Soup E-Commerce, a boutique firm providing web design and e-commerce consulting services to primarily BigCommerce clients.

Prior to launching her own business, Danielle worked at a variety of e-commerce startups in online marketing, merchandising and analytics roles, including as Director of Customer Acquisition and Retention at Shoes.com.

She has also launched several e-commerce businesses of her own, including a subscription dog poop bag company and a hat company for progressive Americans traveling abroad. Her latest venture is 30 Day E-Commerce, a comprehensive do-it-yourself instructional video series for aspiring e-commerce entrepreneurs.

Danielle has published two previous ebooks, _E-Commerce for Everyone: How to Launch a Successful Online Store Using Bigcommerce (or Other Hosted Platforms)_, and _So You Need a Web Designer: How to Find the Right One, Build a Great Working Relationship and Create the Website You Want_, as well as the workbook _Build a Better Password: Create and Save Strong, Secure Passwords the Fun & Easy Way!_

Danielle grew up in Northern Virginia and received a BA in Music with a minor in Women's Studies from Vassar College. She now resides in Los Angeles with her husband Matthew and her dog Lucy.

Made in the USA
Coppell, TX
26 February 2021

50941593R00052